Honeybee's hive

by Clint Twist

Copyright © ticktock Entertainment Ltd 2006
First published in Great Britain in 2006 by ticktock Ltd.,
Unit 2, Orchard Business Centre, North Farm Road, Tunbridge Wells, Kent, TN2 3XF
We would like to thank: Elizabeth Wiggans and Dr John Walters for their help with this book.
ISBN 1 86007 844 3 PB Printed in China
A CIP catalogue record for this book is available from the British Library.

Picture Credits
FLPA Images: 2-3, 8-9 all, 11 all. Science Photo Library: 15r, 17t, 18-19 all, 20b, 21t.
Every effort has been made to trace the copyright holders, and we apologise in advance for any unintentional omissions.
We would be pleased to insert the appropriate acknowledgements in any subsequent edition of this publication.

CONTENTS

What are honeybees?

Honeybees are medium-sized winged insects. They look furry and make honey. They make a distinctive buzzing sound when they fly. They can deliver a painful sting.

How do honeybees live?

Honeybees belong to a sub-group of insects known as social insects because they live in a very large family group called a colony. Most of the honeybees in a colony are workers that collect nectar and pollen from flowers.

Honeybees live in homes called hives.

Where do they live?

Honeybees do not like very cold conditions, and they do not like it very hot and dry. Honeybees live wherever there are plenty of flowers for at least some months of the year.

What do they eat?

Honeybees eat nectar and pollen from flowers, and resin from trees. They have superb flight control, and can check a flower for pollen while hovering in mid-air. This means honeybees can quickly fly on to the next flower.

Understanding minibeasts

Insects belong to a group of minibeasts known as arthropods. Adults have jointed legs but do not have an inner skeleton made of bones. Instead, they have a tough outer "skin" called an exoskeleton that supports and protects their bodies. All adult insects have six legs and most also have at least one pair of wings for flying, although some have two pairs.

Honeybees have two pairs of flying wings.

The Bee up close

The average honeybee worker is about 16mm long and has six legs and two pairs of flying wings. A layer of fine hairs gives this minibeast a furry appearance. It is divided into three parts – head, thorax, and abdomen.

thorax

head

abdomen

A worker honeybee in flight.

The abdomen is largest part of the honeybee's body and contains the digestive system and other important organs.

The head is equipped with antennae, eyes, brain and mouth. The thorax is the middle part of the body with legs and wings.

Inside the upper abdomen, is a special organ called the honey-stomach. Nectar is stored here instead of passing through the digestive system.

Six legs

Bees and other insects are sometimes called hexapods because they have all have six legs (hex means six in Latin). This is correct, but it is not completely accurate. All insects are hexapods, but not all hexapods are insects. A honeybee is an example of a hexapod.

Honeybees have six legs like all other hexapods.

Hive Home

A honeybee colony is a huge family with thousands of closely related members. They build themselves a nest called a hive. The hive is a very busy and highly organized place.

A honeybee nest in Peru.

Honeybees often set up colonies in hollow trees. If no suitable hollows are available they may build a nest on a branch. If trees are in short supply, honeybees will build hives under roofs, on other places on buildings, on the ground, in old termite mounds or below the ground and in caves.

② Most of the other honeybees (about 50,000 per colony) are workers (infertile females).

Every honeybee colony contains three types of honeybee.

(1) There is a single fertile female that does not leave the hive. This is the queen bee.

(3) There are also about 300 male bees called drones. They are smaller than queens, but bigger than workers. They do not contribute to the hive. Their only purpose is to chase after queens on their mating flights.

Treasure House

A hive not only provides a home, it is also the colony's treasure house. As well as the queen bee and the developing larvae, the hive also contains the colony's precious store of food. In order to protect these treasures from being spoiled by bad weather or intruders, worker bees often construct a wall of solid mud around the entire hive.

A bee hive in Malaysia protected by a casing of mud.

Queen Bees

Queen bees are the largest honeybees – about 22 mm long. A queen mates just once, early in adult life. During a mating flight the queen is fertilised by drones from nearby hives. The queen then establishes a new colony.

Fed and cared for by worker bees, the queen lays thousands of eggs a day for the rest of her life. She never leaves the hive again unless there is an emergency such as a flood or forest fire.

A queen bee can control how the eggs develop. Most develop into worker bees. The colony always needs new workers, because most live for just a few months.

Queen bees are the largest bees in the hive.

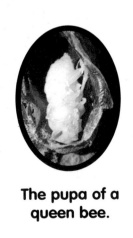

A queen bee inspects a cell in her hive.

The queen occasionally lays eggs that hatch into drones. A queen honeybee will only lay "queen eggs" when the colony needs a new queen because of old age or disease.

The pupa of a
queen bee.

When it is time for a new queen, the old queen lays several queen eggs at the same time. All the eggs receive the same careful treatment, and the first of them to hatch and pupate usually becomes the next queen. The first action of a newly emerged queen is to sting to death all the other potential queens in their cells before they can emerge.

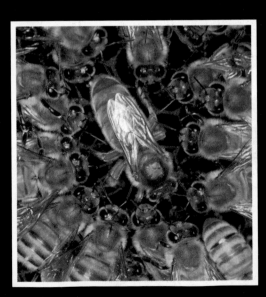

Worker honeybees surrounding a queen honey bee (marked with a pink dot). There is room for just one queen in a hive.

11

cells of Life

T he inside of a hive is a marvellous example of insect architecture and engineering. The queen lays each egg into an individual cell that has been made by the workers from beeswax.

Each cell has six long sides and two neatly shaped ends. They are perfectly designed to fit closely together. After the egg has been laid the cells is capped with wax and sealed.

Inside the hive the queen lays eggs into cells, which are then capped by worker bees.

Inside the cell, the egg hatches into a larva (a caterpillar-like creature). This larva is the juvenile (young) form of a bee. The larvae are fed and cared for by workers that regularly uncap the cells, feed the larvae, and then reseal the cells.

Young bees begin to emerge from capped cells.

Insect Development

Insects develop from eggs in two different ways. With many kinds of insect, including all bees, the eggs hatch into larvae that look very different from the adults. However, with many other kinds of insect, such as cockroaches and grasshoppers, the eggs hatch into nymphs that already have the adult body shape.

When a larva reaches its maximum size, it pupates and forms an outer casing around itself. At this stage in its life a bee is known as a pupa. Inside the casing the pupa changes into the body shape of an adult. A fully formed young bee emerges from the cell.

A selection of European honeybee larvae.

A close-up photograph of a bee pupa.

Repairs & Guard Duty

After a young worker bee emerges from its cell, it spends about a month inside the hive. At first its duties keep it among the cells.

Young workers keep the cells in good repair and also make new ones. Worker bees produce small amounts of wax in special glands on the sides of their abdomens.

A young worker bee repairs cells in a hive. Cells must be kept in good condition for when the queen needs to lay eggs inside them.

They use their legs to scrape this wax into small balls that can be carried around the hive. Young workers chew the wax to make it sticky and use their mouths to shape it and press it into place.

A close-up of the head of a young worker bee.

The youngsters then progress to guard duty. Their job is to keep out intruders that range from insects and other minibeasts to birds and mammals. They flutter their wings at the entrance to help create air currents to keep the inside of the hive cool.

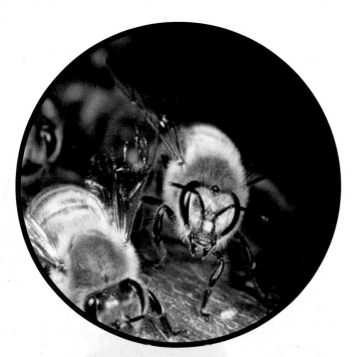

These guard bees are ready to kill any intruder who attempts to enter the hive, losing their own lives in the process.

Sting sacrifice

When a worker honeybee stings an intruder, it sacrifices its life. A bee's sting has barbs that catch on the victim's flesh and hold the sting firmly in place while poison is injected. When the worker moves away after stinging, the sting tears away from its abdomen and is left behind. The unfortunate worker dies soon afterwards.

The used sting of a worker honeybee.

Finding Flowers

Honeybees really like plants with lots of flowers because they produce lots of pollen and nectar. Plants that have flowers must really like honeybees because they do their best to attract them.

Flowers produce pollen so that one flower can fertilise another to produce seeds. Honeybees collect pollen and take it away, accidentally helping the plants by carrying it from flower to flower.

Grains of pollen get lodged among the hairs on the bees' bodies. These then get dislodged in different flowers, resulting in a process called pollination.

A close-up of a flower's pollen grain.

Bees have excellent eyesight; although they can only see in UV light. Flower petals often have patterns designed to attract honeybees, but which are invisible to animals that use ordinary visible light (such as human beings).

The daisy Gaillardia as seen in UV light.

Sweet taste

As if pretty patterns were not enough, many plants also produce small quantities of sweet, sugary nectar, a very high-energy food designed to be especially appealing to insects. Nectar is the favourite food of honeybees.

Honeybees are attracted to flowers because of their nectar.

Doing the Waggle Dance

Each morning that plants are in flower, specially selected scout bees are sent out to find the best sources of pollen and nectar. Any worker can be a scout bee, but usually it is the older, more experienced bees that are chosen.

(**1**) The scout bees fly up to 3 km in all directions from the hive to investigate newly opened flowers. When each scout returns to the hive (left) it reports what it has found using the waggle dance.

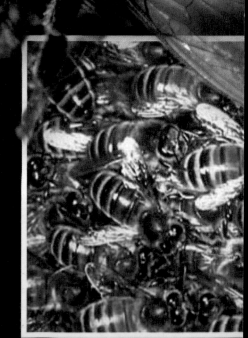

Honeybee navigation

Honeybees navigate (find their way around) by using the sun. Not only do bees use the direction of the sun (it is only rarely directly overhead), but also the height of the sun in the sky, and the strength of sunlight, as it varies during the day. This allows honeybees to know exactly where they are, even when they are out of sight of the hive.

(2) Returning scouts perform a figure-of-eight dance at the hive entrance. The central path of the dance indicates the direction to the food source.

The speed of the dance steps, the number of repetitions, and the speed of the wing fluttering (left) during the dance can all communicate other information, such as the distance, amount and quality of the supply of pollen and nectar.

Honeybees use the sun to find their way to the best flowers, and then trace their way back to the hive.

BUSY Bees

F or the rest of their short lives worker bees collect pollen and nectar every day. This mainly goes to meet the daily demand for food in the hive – the queen and many young bees and larvae must all be fed – although some of this food goes into long-term storage.

Workers collect pollen with their mouths and front legs and carry it back to the hive in special pollen baskets on their back legs. Any nectar that is collected is carried inside a worker's honey-stomach.

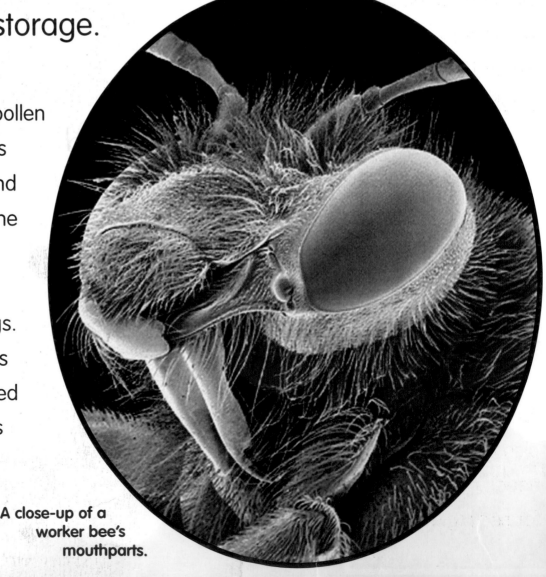

A close-up of a worker bee's mouthparts.

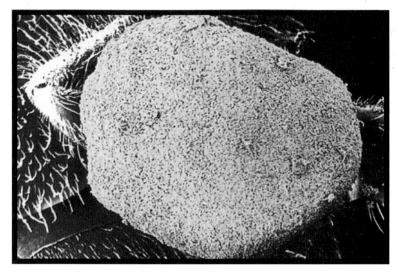

A close-up of a honey bee's pollen basket.

Any food that is not to be consumed immediately is stored in empty egg cells that have been cleaned and resealed. Returning workers squirt any spare nectar in their honey-stomachs into a cell, and add surplus pollen.

Resin from trees such as the Eucalyptus is a vital food source for honeybees.

As well as pollen and nectar, honeybees also collect water (which all animals need), and tree resin, which they use for sealing the ends of the cells.

Honeycombs

Inside the individual wax cells the nectar and pollen mixture slowly dries out into a sticky substance called honey. A collection of close-fitting honey cells is called a comb. This is why we use the word honeycomb to describe any arrangement of closely packed, straight-sided hollow cells.

Honeycomb is made up of hexagonal cells with thin walls.

Honeybees & Humans

Many animals enjoy the taste of honey, and some even enjoy the taste of bees. Human beings like the taste of honey so much that they turned honeybees into farm animals more than 5,000 years ago.

A bee colony can be a purpose-made hive constructed from mud, plaited straw or wood. If the colony is fed when there is no pollen or nectar naturally available, all the stored honey can be removed and the bees will still survive. Honeybees are kept in most countries.

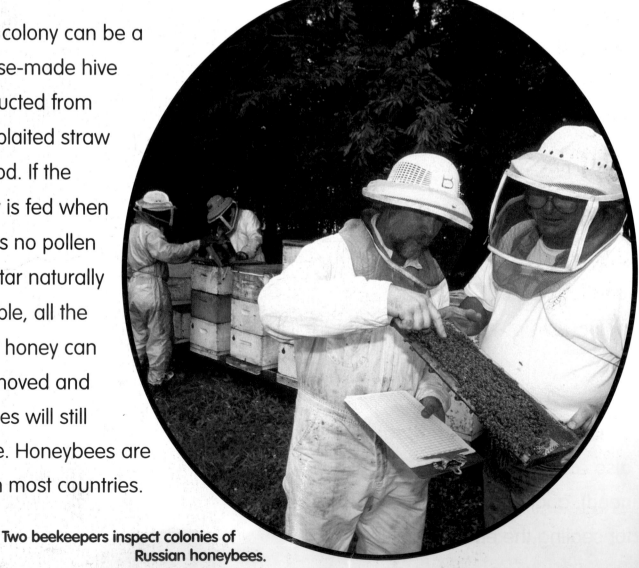

Two beekeepers inspect colonies of Russian honeybees.

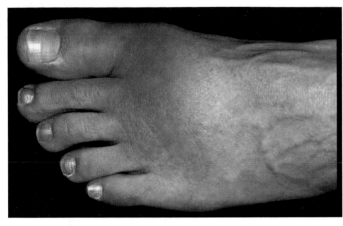

Bee venom injected during an attack causes redness, pain, swelling and itching.

Each beesting contains a very small amount of mild poison, and only very few people are badly affected by a single sting. Lots of stings can deposit enough of the poison to harm a person, however, so beekeepers are always careful. They often wear large hats with a veil to protect their heads and faces.

A beekeeper's hat and veil. Netting provides ventilation and protection against stings.

Candlelight

Beeswax provides people with an additional benefit from honey gathering or beekeeping. For thousands of years, the finest candles have been made from beeswax, which burns brightly and has a pleasing smell. Today, when most candles are made from a wax obtained from crude oil, beeswax is still used for the most expensive and luxurious candles.

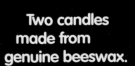

Two candles made from genuine beeswax.

Different Bees

Most bees live in slightly different ways than honeybees. Some live in smaller colonies, and some are solitary creatures. Most of them eat nectar and pollen, but none of them build up such big stores of honey. There are about 40,000 species of bee that scientists know about.

Bumblebees

Most bumblebees are much bigger, hairier and noisier than honeybees. Bumblebees have typical warning colours: black and yellow or black and red. They live in far smaller colonies with a queen and some 20-200 family members in various stages of development. Unlike honeybees, bumblebees are capable of stinging more than once. Only the queen survives the winter. She does this by hibernating in a burrow.

Carpenter Bees

A carpenter bee is about the size of a bumblebee. The female carpenter bee uses the hard point of its sting to chisel out narrow holes in pieces of dead wood. At the bottom of each hole the bee lays a few eggs. Even a single carpenter bee can do a lot of damage to a piece of wooden furniture.

Cuckoo bees

These solitary bees are parasites on other bees. Like the cuckoo birds, cuckoo bees do not build their own nests. Instead, female cuckoo bees search out the nest of another species of solitary bee and invade it. They sting all the eggs and larvae to death before cleaning out the cells so that they can lay their own eggs.

Leaf-cutter bees

Leaf-cutter bees are solitary bees - they live by themselves. They have powerful jaws that are used both for tunnelling into soil and for cutting leaves. After digging a tunnel, the female cuts a series of circular pieces from the leaves of nearby plants. Each piece is rolled into tube and inserted into the tunnel. An egg is laid in this "leaf-cell" before it is sealed up with a store of pollen and nectar to feed the larva after the egg hatches.

Bee Mimics

Identifying different bees is made even more difficult by the fact that lots of other insects want to look like bees – often so they can get inside a hive without being stung by workers on guard at the entrance. Minibeasts that imitate the appearance of bees are known as bee-mimics.

Drone fly
The drone fly belongs to a group of flying insects known as hover flies, many of which are bee or wasp mimics. The drone fly looks just like a harmless honeybee drone, and it tries to sneak into hives to feed on honeybees' stored pollen.

Greater bee fly

The greater bee fly is a fly that looks just like some bee species except that is has a long, extended mouthpart called a proboscis. It uses this proboscis to feed on nectar. Females scatter their eggs while flying around. When the eggs hatch on the ground, the fly larvae seek out the nests of solitary bees and eat the bee larvae.

Velvet ant

This minibeast has the hairy appearance of a bee but, despite its name, is actually a species of wasp. Velvet ants are even more aggressive parasites than cuckoo bees. The female lays her eggs inside the bodies of bee larvae and pupae. When the velvet ant larvae hatch they begin eating the developing bees.

Bumble fly

The bumble fly is one of the hover flies that use their appearance as a means of protection. It feeds on nectar and pollen and relies on predators mistaking it for a real bumblebee. The bumble fly, like other hover flies, has no sting while the bumblebee has a strong, sharp sting.

Find out More
Lifecycle

There are three types of honeybee inside each colony, each with a specific purpose. Queens produce eggs; drones or males mate with a queen from another colony; while workers – non-reproducing females – bring back food. Once an egg hatches into a larva, the type of adult it develops into is determined by what type of food it is fed. A colony usually has just one queen bee. The lifecycle of a honeybee is illustrated in the diagram below.

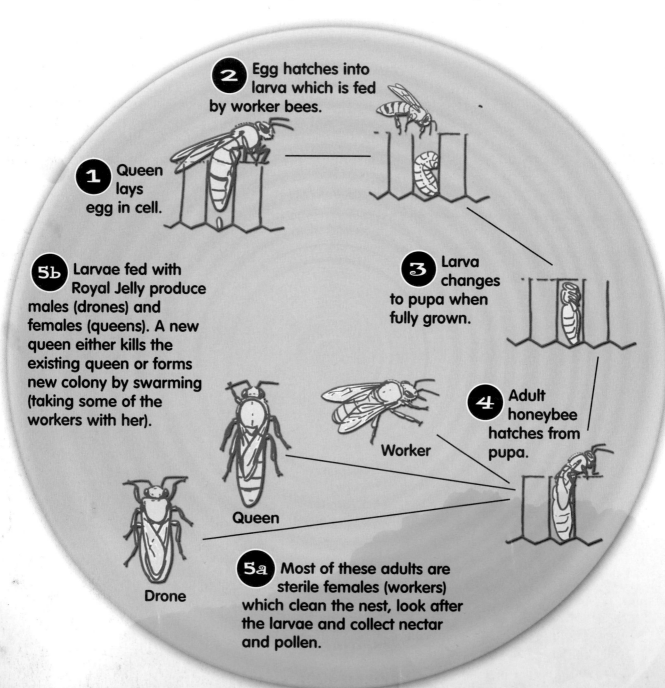

1 Queen lays egg in cell.

2 Egg hatches into larva which is fed by worker bees.

3 Larva changes to pupa when fully grown.

4 Adult honeybee hatches from pupa.

5a Most of these adults are sterile females (workers) which clean the nest, look after the larvae and collect nectar and pollen.

5b Larvae fed with Royal Jelly produce males (drones) and females (queens). A new queen either kills the existing queen or forms new colony by swarming (taking some of the workers with her).

Worker

Queen

Drone

Fabulous Facts

Fact 1: There are about 20,000 species of bees, but only about 4 are considered true honeybees.

Fact 2: Honeybees have been used by people since the age of the pyramids, around 5,000 years ago.

Fact 3: They originated in Tropical Africa and spread from South Africa to Northern Europe and East into India and China.

Fact 4: The first fossil bees date back about 40 million years and are almost identical to modern bees.

Fact 5: Each honeybee colony can have tens of thousands of bees inside. Some colonies contain as many as 80,000 bees.

Fact 6: Larvae hatch from eggs in 3 to 4 days and are fed by worker bees.

Fact 7: A queen may live three to five years; drones usually die before winter; and, workers may live for a few months.

Fact 8: A queen is fed a high protein food produced by young workers which enables her to lay up to 2,000 eggs a day. This is about twice her own weight.

Fact 9: A queen makes only one mating flight during her life. She stores the sperm from up to 20 drones that she collects on that flight. Drones that mate with her die in the act.

Fact 10: Bees eat pollen to produce bee milk, sometimes called royal jelly. They feed this to the queen continuously and to larvae for 3 days after they hatch from eggs.

Fact 11: To make 1 Kg of wax, a bee has to east about 4 Kg of honey. They secrete wax scales from 4 pairs of glands under their abdomen, each wax scale weighing about 1 mg.

Fact 12: The scientist Karl von Frisch studied the behavior of honey bees and was awarded the Nobel Prize for physiology and medicine in 1973. Von Frisch noticed that honey bees communicate with the language of dance.

Fact 13: Larger drone bees have no stings at all. The queen bee has a smooth stinger and could sting multiple times, but the queen does not leave the hive under normal conditions.

GLOSSary

Abdomen – the largest part of an insect's three-part body; the abdomen contains most of the important organs.

Antennae – a pair of special sense organs found at the front of the head on most insects.

Arthropod – any minibeast that has jointed legs; insects and spiders are arthropods.

Beeswax – a sticky, solid substance produced by honeybees and used for building cells.

Cell – a hollow, six-sided structure made by honeybees to raise their young and to store honey.

Colony – a group of insects, or other living things, which live very closely together.

Comb – a collection of cells built side-by-side inside a hive.

Digestive system – the organs that are used to process food.

Drone – a male honeybee; drones are larger that workers but do not have a sting.

Exoskeleton – a hard outer covering that protects and supports the bodies of some minibeasts.

Gland – a part of an animal's body that produces particular substances.

Hive – the nest made by a colony of honeybees.

Honey – sweet, syrupy substance produced by honeybees from pollen and nectar.

Insect – a kind of minibeast that has six legs, most insects also have wings.

Jaws – hinged structures around the mouth that allow some animals to bite and chew.

Larva – a wormlike creature that is the juvenile (young) stage in the life cycle of many insects.

Minibeast – one of a large number of small land animals that do not have a skeleton.

Nectar – a sweet sugary substance produced by flowering plants and used by honeybees to make honey.

Nymph – the juvenile (young) stage in the life cycle of insects that do not produce larvae.

Organ – a part of an animal's body that performs a particular task, e.g. the heart pumps blood.

Parasite – any living thing that lives or feeds on or in the body of another living thing.

Pollen – tiny, multidsided grains that are produced by flowers in order to fertilise other flowers.

Pupa – An insect larva that is in the process of turning into an adult.

Pupation – the process by which insect larvae change their body shape to the adult form.

Queen – the largest honeybee in a colony; the queen is the only female bee that can lay eggs.

Skeleton – an internal structure of bones that supports the bodies of large animals such as mammals, reptiles, and fish.

Thorax – the middle part of an insect's body where the legs are attached.

UV – Ultra violet light that cannot be detected by human eyes, but can be seen by honeybees.

Waggle dance – a pattern of movements used by honeybees to communicate the direction of food sources.

Worker – a sterile female honeybee, nearly all the honeybees in a hive are workers.

INDEX